Contents

What is the environment?

The environment is the world all around us.

We need to care for
the environment.

What is energy?

uses energy

Energy makes many things work.

We can help the environment by saving energy.

Ways to help the environment

We use energy to light our homes.

If we turn off lights we do not
need, we save energy.
We are helping the environment.

We use energy to heat our homes.

If we turn the heating down,
we save energy.
We are helping the environment.

hot water

We use energy to heat water.

If we use less hot water,
we save energy.
We are helping the environment.

A television uses energy.

If we do not leave a television on stand by, we save energy.
We are helping the environment.

A computer uses energy.

If we switch off a computer,
we save energy.
We are helping the environment.

We use energy when we go by car.

If we walk or go by bus,
we save energy.
We are helping the environment.

We can help save energy.

We can help the environment.

How are they helping?

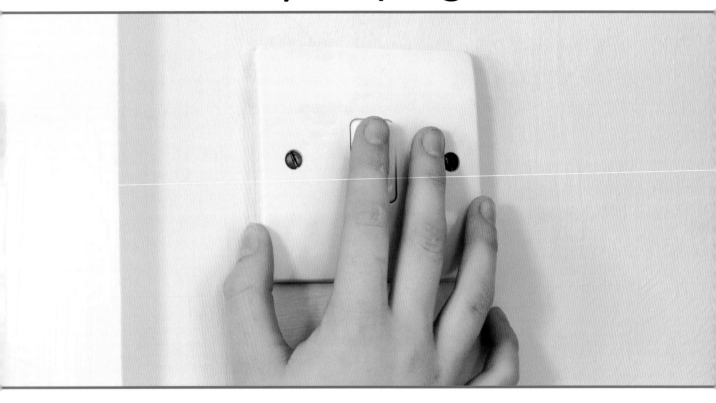

How is this child saving energy?

Answer on p. 24

Picture glossary

energy things like lights, computers and cars need energy to make them work

environment the world around us

Index

Answer to question on p.22: This child is helping to save energy by turning off a light.

Note to Parents and Teachers
Before reading
Talk to children about things that use energy. Explain that we must use energy wisely and not waste it. Talk about how we should be aware of how much energy we use.
After reading
• Look through the pages of a catalogue. Ask the children to identify objects that use energy (TVs, DVD players, iPods, etc.). Cut out the pictures and stick them on a large sheet of paper headed: These things use energy.
• Talk about ways of saving energy, such as using low-energy light bulbs, switching off lights when you leave a room, not leaving the TV on standby. Ask each child to choose one energy-saving method and to draw a picture to illustrate it.
• Play 'Energy Snakes and Ladders'. Tell the children to stand in a line in the middle of a large space – the hall or the playground. If you say something that saves energy they can 'go up a ladder' by jumping forward one, two or three jumps. If you say something that wastes energy they must spiral down a 'snake'. Make statements like: You only use low energy light bulbs – go up 3. You leave the TV on stand by overnight – go down 1. If the children are confident allow one of them to make the statements.